FRANCIS FRITH'S

NEWMARKET TOWN AND CITY MEMORIES

THE FRANCIS FRITH COLLECTION

www.francisfrith.com

FRANCIS FRITH'S

TOWN & CITY
MEMORIES

NEWMARKET

JOAN SHAW was born in Newmarket at the Nursing Home in Cardigan Street, in August 1932. She has a son and daughter, also born in the town. As a child she attended the St Mary's schools in Fitzroy Street, then the Newmarket Grammar School. She gained her Teacher's Certificate at Saffron Walden Teacher Training College and her B.Ed. Hons. degree at the University of East Anglia. Since retiring from the post of Second Deputy Head at Scaltback Middle School in Newmarket, she has pursued her interest in history. From the University of Cambridge Board of Continuing Education, she has obtained a Certificate in Local History and has successfully completed a Certificate in Palaeography for Local and Family Historians.

FRANCIS FRITH'S
TOWN & CITY
MEMORIES

NEWMARKET

JOAN SHAW

FRANCIS FRITH'S
TOWN&CITY
MEMORIES

First published as Newmarket, A Photographic History of your Town
in 2001 by Black Horse Books, an imprint of The Francis Frith Collection
Revised edition published in the United Kingdom in 2006 by
The Francis Frith Collection as Newmarket, Town and City Memories
Limited Hardback Edition ISBN 1-84589-166-X
Paperback Edition ISBN 1-84589-167-8

British Library Cataloguing in Publication Data

Newmarket
Town and City Memories
John Shaw

The Francis Frith Collection®
6 Oakley Business Park, Wylye Road,
Dinton, Salisbury, Wiltshire SP3 5EU
Tel: +44 (0) 1722 716 376
Email: info@francisfrith.co.uk
www.francisfrith.com

Aerial photographs reproduced under licence from Simmons Aerofilms Limited
Historical Ordnance Survey maps reproduced under licence from Homecheck.co.uk

Printed and bound in England

Front Cover: **NEWMARKET, HIGH STREET 1929** 81955t
The colour-tinting in this image is for illustrative purposes only,
and is not intended to be historically accurate

FRANCIS FRITH'S
TOWN & CITY
MEMORIES

Contents

THE MAKING OF AN ARCHIVE

Francis Frith, Victorian founder of the world-famous photographic archive, was a devout Quaker and a highly successful Victorian businessman. By 1860 he was already a multi-millionaire, having established and sold a wholesale grocery business in Liverpool. He had also made a series of pioneering photographic journeys to the Nile region. The images he returned with were the talk of London. An eminent modern historian has likened their impact on the population of the time to that on our own generation of the first photographs taken on the surface of the moon.

Frith had a passion for landscape, and was as equally inspired by the countryside of Britain as he was by the desert regions of the Nile. He resolved to set out on a new career and to use his skills with a camera. He established a business in Reigate as a specialist publisher of topographical photographs.

Frith lived in an era of immense and sometimes violent change. For the poor in the early part of Victoria's reign work was a drudge and the hours long, and ordinary people had precious little free time. Most had not travelled far beyond the boundaries of their own town or village. Mass tourism was in its infancy during the 1860s, but during the next decade the railway network and the establishment of Bank Holidays and half-Saturdays gradually made it possible for the working man and his family to enjoy holidays and to see a little more of the world. With characteristic business acumen, Francis Frith foresaw that these new tourists would enjoy having souvenirs to commemorate their days out. He began selling photo-souvenirs of seaside resorts and beauty spots, which the Victorian public pasted into treasured family albums.

Frith's aim was to photograph every town and village in Britain. For the next thirty years he travelled the country by train and by pony and trap, producing fine photographs of seaside resorts and beauty spots that were keenly bought by millions of Victorians.

THE RISE OF FRITH & CO

Each photograph was taken with tourism in mind, the small team of Frith photographers concentrating on busy shopping streets, beaches, seafronts, picturesque lanes and villages. They also photographed buildings: the Victorian and Edwardian eras were times of huge building activity, and town halls, libraries, post offices, schools and technical colleges were springing up all over the country. They were invariably celebrated by a proud Victorian public, and photo souvenirs – visual records – published by F Frith & Co were sold in their hundreds of thousands. In addition, many new commercial buildings such as hotels, inns and pubs were photographed, often because their owners specifically commissioned Frith postcards or prints of them for re-sale or for publicity purposes.

In order to gain some understanding of the scale of Frith's business one only has to look at the catalogue issued by Frith & Co in 1886: it runs to some 670 pages. By 1890 Frith had created the greatest specialist photographic publishing company in the world, with over 2,000 stockists! The picture on the right shows the Frith & Co display board on the wall of the stockist at Ingleton in the Yorkshire Dales (left of window). Beautifully constructed with a mahogany frame and gilt inserts, it displayed a dozen scenes.

Postcard Bonanza

The ever-popular holiday postcard we know today took many years to appear, and F Frith & Co was in the vanguard of its development. Postcards became a hugely popular means of communication and sold in their millions. Frith's company took full advantage of this boom and soon became the major publisher of photographic view postcards.

Francis Frith died in 1898 at his villa in Cannes, his great project still growing. His sons Eustace and Cyril continued their father's monumental task, expanding the number of views offered to the public and recording more and more places in Britain, as the coasts and countryside were opened up to mass travel. The archive Frith created

continued in business for another seventy years. By 1970 it contained over a third of a million pictures of 7,000 cities, towns and villages. The massive photographic record Frith has left to us stands as a living monument to a special and very remarkable man.

This book shows Newmarket as it was photographed by this world-famous archive at various periods in its development over the past 150 years. Every photograph was taken for a specific commercial purpose, which explains why the selection may not show every aspect of the town landscape. However, the photographs, compiled from one of the world's most celebrated archives, provide an important and absorbing record of your town.

FROM THE AIR

NEWMARKET FROM THE AIR 1920 AF1754

INTRODUCTION

INTRODUCTION

NEWMARKET is a thriving, busy town. Besides being a market town, it is the headquarters of horse racing and is establishing itself as a tourist centre. Close proximity to the A14 enables it today to serve as a dormitory town. A 1945 map would have shown only a quarter of the development we find here today. It was a relatively late town, established around 1200 AD. Its area was only 570 acres, whereas its parent parishes of Exning and Woodditton were approximately 5,000 acres each. The parish of St Mary's, which is on the north side of the High Street, was carved from Exning in Suffolk, and All Saints' on the south side from Woodditton in Cambridgeshire. In area the latter is the slightly larger parish.

Newmarket does not appear in the Domesday Book. Its siting along a series of springs and a small stream was due to the business acumen of Richard d'Argentien, the recipient of the St Mary's acreage when he married Cassandra de Insula (de L'Isle), receiving it as a marriage portion in the 1190s. Once the market was established, small crofts and houses were built. The townspeople seem to have been free tenants, not owing work to the Lord of the Manor, but paying rent, taxes and fines. The St Mary's side developed behind the High Street quite early in the town's existence, for it had the weekly Tuesday market in its parish. All Saints' grew during the Stuart period; both James I and Charles II erected 'palaces' here (see 88441, page 12), and the aristocracy built their own residences during the late 17th and 18th centuries.

The real development occurred with the arrival of the railway in 1848, which was situated beyond the town boundary. Many of the terraced houses built specifically for the railway workers still exist today. Until the Duke of

High Street 1922 71913

INTRODUCTION

Left: PALACE HOUSE 1938 88441

The only part of King Charles II's palace to survive is incorporated in this 19th-century red brick house, Palace House, owned at the time of this photograph by Lord Rothschild. The house is situated in Palace Street; the entrance was reached by an elegant set of stone steps. The sash windows had blinds which were only raised when it was occupied, usually on race days. Neat iron railings and a gate separated the gardens from the pavement. A globe-shaped light illuminated the entrance. Neglected in the latter half of the 20th century, the house was purchased in the 1990s by the local council. It has been renovated and is now the impressive Tourist Information Centre.

Portland ploughed the Cambridge Heath and set it with grass in the early 19th century, the prehistoric trackways across the heathland leading to neighbouring villages, and known collectively as the Icknield Way, were visible. The Icknield Way ran from Norfolk along the chalk ridge to Wessex, passing through what today is called Newmarket. The village parish boundaries are very ancient and meet along the trackway. To the north are the fen-edge villages of Bottisham, the Swaffhams, Burwell, Exning and Snailwell. On the south side are the boulder clay villages of Brinkley, Westley Waterless, Dullingham, Stetchworth, Woodditton, Cheveley, Ashley and Moulton. They all had access to and from this important trackway, which was vital to their prosperity. Newmarket was situated on the old great London to Norwich road. It was the gateway to East Anglia: roads branched in several directions, leading to Ely, Bury St Edmunds, Cambridge, Thetford, Brandon and Haverhill, all about a day's journey away. By 1472 there were at least seventeen named alehouses in Newmarket, catering for travellers just as their replacements do today.

In the early 17th century, Newmarket was described as a 'great thorowfare' and later as a 'well built street seated in the Great Road, full of inns'. The Stuarts loved Newmarket; King James I first came here in 1605. It is thanks to the Stuarts and successive Royal connections that Newmarket is now famous throughout the world as a centre for racing, training, breeding and the sale of racehorses.

THE CLOCK TOWER C1950 N23002

*As indicated by the sign-posts, the Clock Tower
forms a focal point in the district.*

HIGH STREET - NORTH SIDE & BOTTOM

IF we stand at what is known locally as the bottom of the High Street, the Jubilee Clock Tower is just visible in the distance. Beyond it is the old toll road leading to Bury St Edmunds and Norwich. Today it still marks the top of the east end of the High Street.

The road is very wide, which was convenient when animals and geese were herded through the town on their way to London and a cattle market was held in the

town. In 1922 the High Street did not have white lines to guide the traffic (see 71913, pages 10-11). The sloping cobbles between the pavement and the road were used for the market stalls on Tuesday and Saturday, and the parking of cars or carts on other days. It is obvious that the photograph was not taken on a race day or market day, as reports of congestion on these days were frequent around this period. Outside the White Hart Hotel

Left: THE WHITE HART 1922 DETAIL FROM 71913

The White Hart is an imposing stone-faced building of the Regency period; it appears on the 1787 plan of Newmarket. An alehouse stood here in the 15th century, so possibly parts of the interior were older than this façade. In the 19th century the owners were brewers as well as innkeepers. The London to Norwich coach made a refreshment stop here. It was a popular place with the better-off racegoers in the 1920s. In Kelly's Directory of 1937 it belonged to Trust Houses Ltd.

Opposite: THE WHITE HART
C1960 N23046

Unfortunately, the White Hart received a direct hit on 18 February 1941, when a lone raider bombed the north side of the High Street. After the war it was rebuilt in the style of the building between the inn and the Memorial Hall; it blends in with the immediate vicinity very well. During the past few years it has again been altered, and the lower windows have been enlarged. It is still a popular venue for inhabitants and visitors alike.

(on page 14) stands an Austin car; it has a luggage rack and spoked wheels. It closely resembles a brougham carriage, but with an engine instead of horses. On page 11 we can see a horse-drawn vehicle standing by the Post Office. The hours of business were 8.00am to 7.00pm on weekdays and 9.00am to 10.30am on Sundays. On the right a van appears to be making deliveries to Lakemans, the timber-framed building, which was a baker and confectioner's shop. The clothes are very varied; the girls passing The White Hart on

their 'sit up and beg' bicycles are more in keeping with the flapper age, whereas the lady with the child outside Boots and the lady opposite to her on the other side of the road appear to be wearing Edwardian clothes. Everyone has a hat to complete their outfit.

Beyond the White Hart, the shops all have sun blinds to protect their commodities, a common practice until fairly recent times. They are all set in old 17th-, 18th- or 19th-century houses which can still be identified in some

Above Left: HIGH STREET, THE POST OFFICE C1960 DETAIL FROM N23042

The Post Office shown here was built after the war on the site of Willoughby House; the brickwork matches that of The Jockey Club.

Above Right: HIGH STREET, THE POST OFFICE 1922 71913B

The Post Office and the Telephone Exchange were housed in a building which was reputed to be the Feathers Inn in the 17th century. It was always a busy place. As can be seen here, there appear to be more people in front of the post office than any where else in the High Street. Unfortunately, the fifth bomb that fell on 18 February 1941 destroyed the building completely. It also effectively destroyed the communications of Newmarket, which was very serious for the Forces here. The majority of the 27 fatalities that day occurred in the Post Office. The King Edward VII Memorial Hall was requisitioned for the duration of the war to serve as the Post Office, and after the war a splendid new one was built on the south side of the High Street opposite the White Hart.

cases today, except for those destroyed in 1941. The houses remain, although the lower floors are now shops. Church Lane, a very old lane, comes next, then a small tobacconist sharing a converted house with one of the few chain stores, Boots Cash Chemists (Eastern) Ltd, telephone No 152; the Boots neon sign can be seen plainly in 71913. The building with the lowest roof line is Rothsay House, occupied by Osmond Griffiths, auctioneer, valuer, house and estate agent, telephone No 55. In the early 19th century Rothsay House was owned by William Crockford, the famous London gaming-house owner; he had a very successful gambling club here, called Crockford's Coffee House. Then comes New Cut, which covers the old stream; it is known today as No 1 drain. It is reputed that it was originally covered following orders from Charles II to provide a sewer. Today it is the drain for storm water. The next building is the old Post Office (see 71913B).

HIGH STREET C1960 N23039

The King Edward VII Memorial Hall served as the Post Office after the raid in 1941. It was erected in 1914 on the site of the King's House, which had to be demolished to make room for it. The Hall is a red brick building with stone dressings. It has served as a venue for meetings, shows, clubs, dances and indoor markets. Today it is the Town Hall for the Newmarket Town Council.

HIGH STREET - SOUTH SIDE & BOTTOM

THE wide High Street had to be crossed at one's own risk, and the young ladies on their bicycles have plenty of room to cycle side by side (see 71912, page 20). The street was well-paved, and was supplied with both gas and electric lighting. The gas was supplied by the Newmarket Gas Co and the electricity by the Newmarket Electric Light Co Ltd; both were situated in Exning Road. The first house on the right of 71912 is on the Newmarket Plan of 1787; it was an elegant-looking house at this period. Next is Willoughby House; then comes the range of buildings that comprised the Jockey Club. Just visible, with a sunblind, is a very high-class leather shop, H W Hill. Until recent years, when it closed, it was the aim of many people to own a leather suitcase from this shop. Hill's had clients from all over the world. Race and sale days were always extremely busy for them. The tall building with the gable has been a clothes and haberdasher's shop since the 19th century, under various names. Today it is a complex of several units, still providing similar goods needed by the inhabitants of the town. The couple standing front right are at the junction of the Avenue and the High Street.

If the couple on the right of 71912 had turned to their left, they would have been in The Avenue (71926, page 25), which led to the passenger station. In the early 20th century Newmarket had three railway stations: the oldest one, in Old Station Road, was used to transport racehorses, and the newest was the passenger station.

18

THE JOCKEY CLUB ROOMS 1922 71922

The frontage was quite spectacular with the cut stone and the sash windows. The entrance on the left that resembles Greek architecture leads to the Subscription Rooms, now the National Horseracing Museum. A lone van with spoked wheels passes by: on the side is painted 'WHM Collis Browne, 'Highfield', Saxon St'.

HIGH STREET - SOUTH SIDE & BOTTOM

It opened in 1901, and the area we see here was still being developed. The advent of this station made the second station, at Warren Hill, Bury Road, virtually obsolete, as it had been constructed to relieve the congestion on race-days. The new station was nearer than either of the others to the racecourses. The old Baroque-style station was demolished in 1981, despite many protests.

The street light hangs above the centre of the road (71926, page 24), and is apparently anchored to either side. The lime trees lining both sides of the road are beautiful mature trees today. The car is heading down the centre of the road towards the High Street. King Edward VII Memorial Hall is in the distance, facing the Avenue.

The Jockey Club Rooms,
The King's Entrance 1922 71924

HIGH STREET - SOUTH SIDE & BOTTOM

Left: HIGH STREET 1922 71912

Below: THE JOCKEY CLUB ROOMS 1922 71923

Several members of the Jockey Club, including Royalty, had suites of rooms here. They are still used today.

HIGH STREET - SOUTH SIDE & BOTTOM

THE JOCKEY CLUB 1938 88440

The Jockey Club was designed in the neo-Georgian style in the early 1930s by the professor of architecture at the Bartlett School of Architecture, Professor Sir Albert E Richardson. It is the headquarters of the club. The building has two storeys, with a five-window main range deeply recessed between two wings of three windows each, which are canted. The prominent central copper-clad rotunda on eight Doric columns can be seen above the hipped, pantiled roofs. One of three arches which form an arcade is just visible.

Details Clockwise From Top Left:
GLOBE LIGHT, PALACE HOUSE 1938 88441
SUSPENDED STREET LIGHT 1922 71926
STREET LIGHT 1922 71912
HIGH STREET LIGHT 1938 88436

High Street - South Side & Bottom

Left: HIGH STREET, PANTON HOUSE 1922
DETAIL FROM 71912

The large house at the junction of the Avenue and the High Street has had an interesting history. Although it had become three houses by 1922, it was originally built as one large one. It has a stone frontage which was added at some time to make it look more fashionable, but behind this façade is an 18th-century red brick house. The wings at either end still have interior 18th-century alcoves, doors, stairs and ceiling mouldings.

Above Right: THE AVENUE
1922 71926

Right: HIGH STREET 1929 81956

Traffic does not appear to have increased, although white lines are now on the road. The conversing ladies seem to be oblivious to the fact that they are on the road. The placards outside the King Edward VII Memorial Hall have not caught their attention. The new Kinema is showing a comedy.

High Street 1938 88436

Traffic has increased greatly by now. A public telephone box has been installed on the left, and the street lights on both sides of the road have been modernised. The Kinema has become the Kingsway, and is showing a double feature, 'Second Best Bed' with Tom Walls and 'Tarzan's Revenge', starring Glen Morris. The adjacent shop, Currys, is advertising cycles and radios.

High Street - South Side & Bottom

HIGH STREET - SOUTH SIDE & BOTTOM

In the 1740s, Thomas Panton senior lived and trained at Panton House, on the corner of the Avenue and the High Street (71912, page 24). He was 'Keeper of the King's running horses at Newmarket' to King George II. His son, 'Polite' Tommy Panton, was one of the first stewards of the Jockey Club, and was Keeper of the racehorses at Newmarket to George III; his sister Mary married the Duke of Ancaster. The house had a pleasure garden, and there were numerous service rooms and elegant living areas. It was sold at Panton's death in 1809 to William Crockford, who had made a fortune from his famous London Gambling Club. Sold at Crockford's death in 1844, it was divided into three houses. One, on the corner of The Avenue, was the residence of Lady Cardigan, and became known as Cardigan Lodge; her husband played a major role in the charge of the Light Brigade. In the 1880s a solicitor, William Parr Isaacson, lived in Willoughby House. He wrote several dramas, at least one of which was performed in the Fisher Theatre in the town. The 20th century saw the centre house becoming an entertainment venue. It has served as a cinema (called the Kinema and then the Kingsway), a bingo hall, and several night clubs; at one time it was known as Club 'M'.

The Jockey Club was formed in London in the 1750s to construct a set of rules to govern racing; it moved permanently to Newmarket in 1771. The members took over a coffee shop and its adjacent buildings on the High Street; a disastrous fire in the early 1930s destroyed many old features. Professor Sir Albert Richardson was employed to design the new Jockey Club. He built it around the original Georgian coffee shop room, and created an impressive neo-Georgian building which holds a prominent place in the High Street today. The old Subscription Rooms have been converted into the National Racehorse Museum, which Her Majesty the Queen opened on 30 April 1983.

Above Left: HIGH STREET c1960 N23042

Traffic has increased so much that a pedestrian crossing has been installed from the White Hart to the Post Office, and cars are parked on both sides of the road. The street lights are much larger than in the 20s and 30s, and their light is directed on to the road.

Left: THE JOCKEY CLUB AND THE POST OFFICE c1955 N23028

The Jockey Club, the headquarters of racing, has an imposing frontage. It extends back to Cardigan Street, and includes offices, a residential block, a royal suite, gardens and lawns. The new Post Office complements it perfectly. A road-sweeper is sweeping in front of the Jockey Club; his barrow stands on the extreme left.

SUFFOLK COUNTY MAP

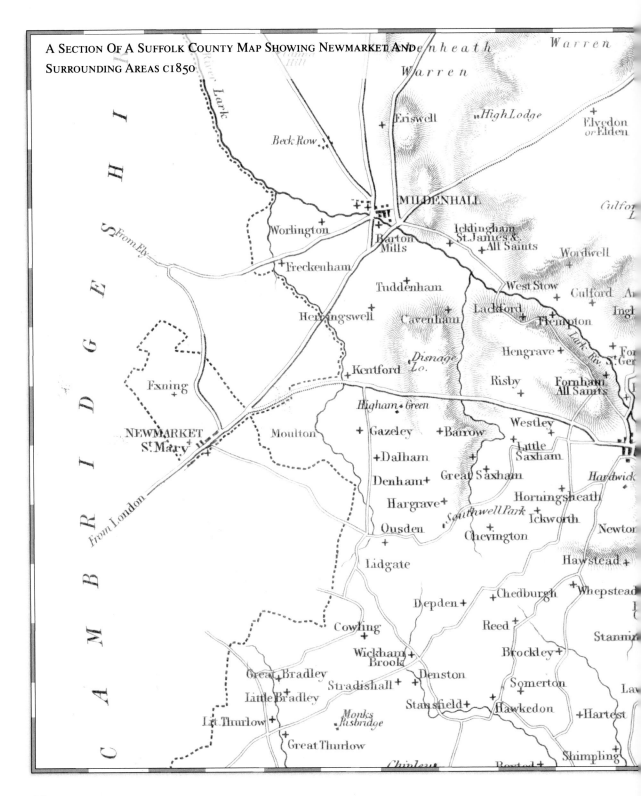

A SECTION OF A SUFFOLK COUNTY MAP SHOWING NEWMARKET AND SURROUNDING AREAS c1850

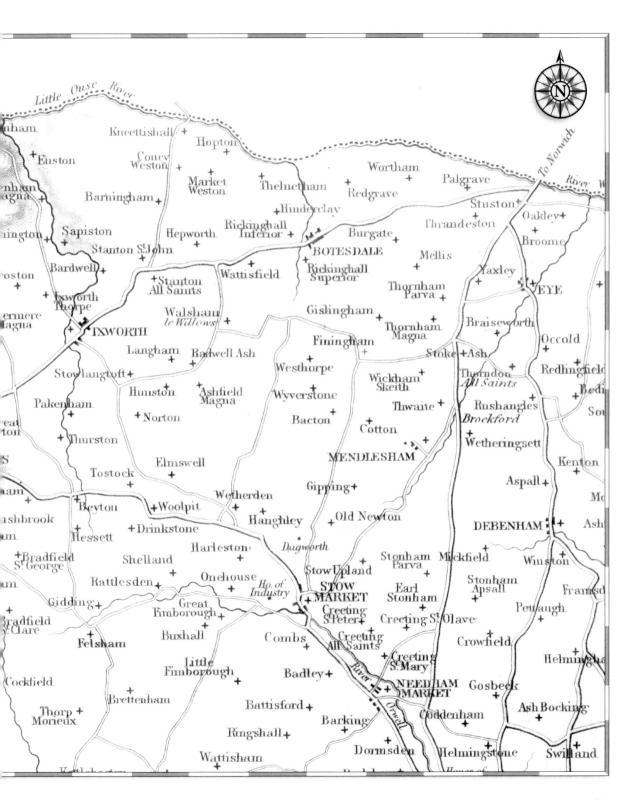

HIGH STREET - CENTRE

ON the north side of the street, (81955, left) is a stableman leaning on his cycle. He has the customary cap on his head, and a sports jacket or a hacking-jacket; his trousers are either inside riding boots or leather gaiters, which were also part of the stableman's outfit. From his mouth dangles a cigarette. He would not be smoking if he was riding a horse, as he could be suspended or even sacked if he was caught smoking whilst riding. A policeman looks on from his precarious place in the middle of the road. His white gloves show up very clearly; he is possibly standing at the cross-roads to direct the traffic. A delivery bicycle is outside J W Carr's the chemist (near left); it leans against a hitching post. Inside Carr's there was a high shelf with large pottery containers - one

It is Market Day. Stalls can be seen on both sides of the High Street. Many stall holders come from nearby villages with their home-grown produce, just as the first market traders would have done in the 13th century. There are many men in town today; the majority are wearing caps. This was the usual thing for jockeys and stablemen to wear until recent years, when the Health and Safety Regulator introduced hard hats for riders to wear.

of them was labelled 'Leeches'. The largest advertisement in the street is a banner hanging above the sun-blinds. proclaiming 'all Kodak supplies'.

Across the entrance to Wellington Street (just past Carr's, on the left) a group of men are chatting, possibly about racing and the chances of a Newmarket horse that was running that day. The old shop on the other side is Sheppard & Co, grocers, where sugar was weighed and put into blue bags and there was always the smell of newly-ground coffee near the door.

The prestigious Craven Club had rooms in the Carlton Hotel building (see 81955, page 34). Fred Astaire, who had a horse in training with Jack Leach, was a member of this Club in the 1920s, and came here when he was performing at the Palace Theatre, London. Forces were billeted here during the war, and in the 1950s it became the Carlton. The ballroom was used for many and varied dances, from local hops to the hunt balls. The Winter Garden had a fountain in it which came from a natural spring; when the modern Boots was built here, it was reported at the time that tons of concrete were used to suppress the spring.

Left: THE CARLTON HOTEL 1929 detail from 81955

The Carlton Hotel had a prominent place in the High Street; it was a very popular venue for the town and surrounding district. The Greyhound posting inn stood on this site for most of the 19th century. In 1897 it became the Victoria Mansions. It was converted and rebuilt with 70 rooms and 12 large self-contained apartments, designed to appeal to wealthy racehorse owners and top jockeys. The total floor area was 45,000 square feet. Built in the French Empire style, it had a typically ornate frontage. The building was constructed of red brick with Bath stone dressings; its first floor balcony can be seen in the photograph. The five floors were topped by a mansard roof with a domed cupola. There was a large lift from the first floor and the wide stairway was of Purbeck marble.

Many people can still remember the dances and other functions held here. During the war, the American Red Cross used part of it for a club for the American forces stationed in the area. The local ladies who joined the organisation learnt how to make American doughnuts (the cake type with a hole in the middle), which were drenched with sugar and prized greatly by local people if they were given one. The Carlton was demolished in 1977.

If we look across the road, the front of Golding's shop can be seen beyond the Star (81955, pages 32-33, opposite the Carlton). It was a family business that was only sold quite recently; the name carries on. White's Suffolk Directory of 1885 has this entry: 'Golding Samuel, draper, outfitter, hatter & boot dir. High Street'. All kinds of racing and riding clothes are still made, and are sent to customers all over the world.

The Star can be seen next, an old inn which can be traced back to the 16th century. The 1674 Hearth Tax return shows that it had 20 hearths, making it one of Newmarket's largest dwellings. An inventory for 1669 is extant, and the rooms can still be identified today. The front of the inn was on the High Street, while its buildings ran the length of Sun Lane and the Tap Room opened onto Palace Street, up to its closure in the post-war years. The Star's black sign is clearly visible. The sash windows have drip mouldings, which are both useful and decorative. The coach entrance to the yard can be seen, and so can the three garret windows. Several men and women are walking or standing in the entrance to Sun Lane. Then comes the Black Horse, another popular hostelry; it has several bicycles propped up against it. The Black Horse too has a sign with its name on it.

A N Lakeman is next (near right); it is a timber-framed medieval building with tiny tiles on the roof, possibly part of the complex that James I used. There are three entrances. The first door leads to a living area, the second to the restaurant and tea-room, and the corner entrance leads to the shop. Here you can buy freshly-baked bread, iced buns, fancy buns and cakes of all descriptions. There is a balcony over the shop from the living quarters. The heart-shaped lamps have Lakeman on them, and on the wall above the restaurant door is painted 'afternoon tea'. The sign over the shop entrance has a particularly attractive ornate bracket, and there is a cover over the cakes inside the window. The shop is on a junction with a pedestrian way which was and is called Kingston Passage; it leads through to Park Lane.

On the other side of the street from the Carlton was Musk & Co (see N23003), an eminent butcher

HIGH STREET - CENTRE

HIGH STREET C1955 N23005

The market is still held in the High Street at this time, but fewer blinds are visible on the shops. The Maypole (left) is on the ground floor of a building which had survived the rationing and the bombing. Elaines, a very popular hairdressers (left), is in the apartments above the grocers. As we look towards the clock tower, it is rather disconcerting to see that a small car by the stalls seems to be travelling towards the oncoming traffic. The street is wider than it was in the 1920s; the parking and market space is not as roomy. Simpsons, beyond the Maypole, had been established for many years as a printer, stationer and bookseller; the shop had an elaborately designed old frontage. This was unfortunately destroyed when it was sold a few years ago; the shop is now totally featureless. It was from here that the local paper, the 'Newmarket Journal', was produced - it was a monthly publication in 1872 and a weekly one in 1882, and it is still published today. The shop sells newspapers, magazines, books, all types of stationery and souvenirs. The Carlton next door is selling draught Bass. Goldings and Son, the tailors, are prominent on the other side of the street.

and sausage maker who held three Royal Warrants. Newmarket butchers have long been famous for their sausages. The shop is now the Nationwide Building Society; the impressive tiled front is still there, and has a preservation order on it. J Ward & Sons, next door, sold cycles, toys and electrical goods including televisions sets;

towering above the International Stores beyond is the Congregational chapel.

The Congregational chapel was erected in 1863, at a cost of upwards of £3,500. It stood on the site of the old palace of King Charles II. Its dedication was in commemoration of those Nonconformists who suffered persecution for

HIGH STREET C1955 N23003

There is still little evidence that the street is busy with traffic, which is probably just as well. Vehicles are parked in odd places, and the one coming up the High Street appears to be travelling in the middle of the road. A man in the foreground seems to be inspecting his motorcycle. The Carlton dominates the street behind him. The lofty cupola stands proudly against the skyline; this magnificent Victorian edifice was beloved by most local inhabitants and loathed by many purist architects.

their faith. The building was in the Gothic style. It had a main structure and a separate clock tower surmounted by a weather vane. Designed to accommodate 650, its oak pulpit and seating were made of timber from the old palace. This too has been demolished.

The market is no longer held on the High Street. A new Market Square was created when the Rookery, a modern shopping precinct, was created in the latter part of the 20th century. It functions on Tuesdays and Saturdays on the St Mary's side of the town. Both Wellington Street and Market Street lead directly to the Rookery and the market place.

THE EAST END, OR TOP END, OF THE HIGH STREET

HIGH STREET, FROM THE GOLDEN LION C1955 N23024

This handsome white rendered building, with its Regency windows, has the remains of a cockpit in the basement dating from at least the time of Charles II. During that period there were several cockpits in the town; this one, however, is very close to the palace - the entrance to Palace Street is directly in front of the lorry on the right. The building served as a theatre from the late 18th to the 19th century: the famous Fisher family of Norwich had it on their circuit, and there are extant play bills for 1831 and 1845 in the Fisher Collection at Wells-next-the-Sea. Some of the earliest films to come to the town were shown here. It also served as a Town Hall for a short period, and has also housed several shops, including the Gas Company. Today it is the fashion shop 'Jane'. It stretches back a considerable way and is very roomy.

THE EAST END, OR TOP END, OF THE HIGH STREET

MOST of the shops at the top end of the High Street are set in 18th-century houses, making this an attractive corner of the town. On the left of N23062, pages 42-43, is Barrow, a chemist's. In White's Suffolk Directory of 1885 it was owned by Frank Barrow, chemist and druggist. His brother William Barrow, MRCVS, practised veterinary surgery from the same address. The Crown Hotel next door can be traced back by extant documents to 1577. During the 19th century it was a carriers, sending goods to London and Bury St Edmunds. The public house is still there today, continuing to supply sustenance to locals and visitors alike; during this period it was selling Steward & Patterson beer. On the other side of the street, at the junction with Rous Road, is Gilbert & Son, saddlers. They made saddles, harness and other leather goods for horses; they also made jockey silks.

Their clientele was world-wide. Today their shop can be found in Queensbury Road, close to Tattersalls, the famous auctioneers of racehorses. The large building on this side of the junction incorporates part of the Old Red Lion. Richardson's, right, is a shop for babies' clothes and underwear; the personal attention once received there is what we often lack in service today. The Black Cat also occupies an old building. Its sign boasts that teas are available and that everything is home made. The building on the near corner (see also N23024) has a long and interesting history.

A Mobilgas tanker can be seen passing by the clock tower (see N23062, centre rear). The pram being pushed past the post box and the telephone box was in the height of fashion; today, smaller manoeuvrable types are used so that they can easily be put into vehicles.

HIGH STREET C1960 N23040

On the north side of the High Street we see Layngs the grocers, the 17th-century Bull, Barclays Bank, Tindall the stationers, Lloyd's Bank, the Golden Lion, Woolworths and Cartwright & Son.

THE EAST END, OR TOP END, OF THE HIGH STREET

THE CLOCK TOWER c1960 N23062

This end of the town is dominated by the Jubilee Clock Tower. It was built in 1889, at a cost of £600, at the junction of the High Street and the Bury and Old Station roads. It is of red brick with stone dressings; on each side at the base are drinking water fountains. It contains a Derby clock given by Charles Blanton Esquire, the trainer of a famous racehorse, Robert the Devil.

THE EAST END, OR TOP END, OF THE HIGH STREET

The buildings surrounding the Clock Tower are virtually unaltered in pictures 88438, N23029, N23067 and N23068, pages 48-51; the shops have changed usage and names, but the buildings are constant. Today the Jubilee Clock Tower can be seen and approached more easily again. The roundabout has gone, and a series of islands and roadways contain and direct the traffic. Apart from the loss of the four standard lamp posts, the Clock Tower looks more in keeping with its original position now than in any era since 1929.

Photograph 71915, pages 52-53, shows the view from the Clock Tower looking down the High Street. The tall timber-framed building on the right is The Chestnuts, one of the few houses in the High Street that has remained residential. Covered in Virginia creeper, it makes a colourful splash on autumnal days. Cycle racks are provided by many shops at this period, as we can see outside the shop with the striped blind. Across the road two policemen are conversing. They are near the entrance to Rous Road, about 500 yards from the Police Station.

The most imposing building here is the Rutland Arms, the large inn facing the Clock Tower (also see the detail from N23001, page 55).

HIGH STREET c1960 N23045

44

THE EAST END, OR TOP END, OF THE HIGH STREET

The Rutland Arms stands on the site of a medieval alehouse. Before the rebuilding and refurbishing of the inn, its name was the Ram. This story about the inn is reputed to be true: in 1750, the eccentric Lord Orford was crossing the Bury heath in his coach, which was pulled by a team of four stags. Unfortunately, the Essex hounds out on the heath got the scent of the stags. Lord Orford rode full gallop into the Ram yard, where an ostler slammed and barred the gate to the inn and so saved the stags.

The Duke of Rutland was Lord of the Manor of Newmarket when the Rutland Arms was constructed. It is regarded as a most successful and well-planned building. Designed by John Kent in 1815, it is a substantial red brick inn. The façade is pure Georgian. The lovely sash windows on the first floor are similar to those of the old Town Hall, which it faces. The High Street façade is almost three times the length of the entrance frontage. The large coach arch leads into a cobbled courtyard, which we can just see in N23001, page 55; also see 71930, page 54.

On the left of N23025, page 54, we can see the exit arch for coaches leaving the Rutland Arms. The entrance was the front arch on Rutland Hill. The shop next to the inn is a flower shop; on a 1787 plan of Newmarket it is shown as a coffee house. The adjacent shop is Quants, a quality shoe shop with an excellent reputation. Wiggs the Jewellers comes next; the family business has been here for well over 100 years. The tiled frontage of Musk & Co, the butchers, stands out amongst the plain glass frontages.

THE JUBILEE CLOCK TOWER 1929 81957

This photograph was taken from the Bury Road. There is plenty of room for traffic and people. The tower has four very substantial lights to illuminate it. At night, with the clock lit from inside and the coloured windows illuminated, it must have been a welcome sight to those returning home to Newmarket from the eastern direction. Near the clock tower is the Jubilee Café (left), supplying food and drink to hungry and thirsty travellers.

THE EAST END, OR TOP END, OF THE HIGH STREET

THE CLOCK TOWER 1938 88438

This time we see the Clock Tower from The Exeter Road. It has iron railings around it to form a roundabout. Keep Left signs are instructing road users what to do. The weather-vane with the racehorse can be seen plainly against the sky.

THE EAST END, OR TOP END, OF THE HIGH STREET

Then come Wards and the International Stores. The roofs of the Congregational Chapel can be seen; its shrubbery spills over onto the pavement on the left.

There are a variety of vehicles here - four vans, a delivery lorry, bicycles and several cars. A bus stop has been established next to the first lamp standard on the right. There are two islands for pedestrians: one is at the crossroad junction in the middle of the High Street, and one by the Post Office.

The high chimney stacks in N23064, page 55, are eye-catching, rivalling the Carlton cupola for attention. Chadwicks, the first shop on the right, is using the sunblind for advertising its flowers and fruit. The Waggon & Horses & Market House Inn is a lovely old building. There are two doors with rather flamboyant Corinthian capitals above the pillars and elaborate console brackets by the windows. It is basically 16th-century, with 18th- and 19th-century additions. Until well after the Second World War, the cattle market was held in the Waggon & Horses yard on Tuesdays. There were pens for cattle, sheep and pigs, and there was an abattoir here. At the time of this photograph, the inn sold Whitbread beer to the customers.

THE ROUNDABOUT C1960 N23068

A policeman contemplates the traffic tower.

THE JUBILEE CLOCK TOWER C1955 N23029

This view was taken from The Bury Road. The roundabout has many bushes growing on it; the area is no longer accessible to the public at this time. The illuminated Keep Left signs also have directional arrows.

The East End, or Top End, of the High Street

THE ROUNDABOUT, FROM SNAILWELL ROAD C1960 N23067

Traffic has obviously increased by the time of this photograph. Many people are now coming to the race meetings in cars, and the railway is in decline. The police have erected a traffic control tower inside the roundabout: this enables them to direct the traffic with temporary lights on race days.

The East End, or Top End, of the High Street

High Street 1922 71915

THE EAST END, OR TOP END, OF THE HIGH STREET

The East End, or Top End, of the High Street

THE EAST END, OR TOP END, OF THE HIGH STREET

HIGH STREET C1960 N23064

Above Left: HIGH STREET C1955 N23025

Left: THE RUTLAND HOTEL, THE INNER COURTYARD 1922 71930

The Clock Tower is visible through the arch. Over the inside of the archway are a set of service bells; servants could not make the excuse that they were working outside and could not hear the guests summoning them. The bells are numbered between 12 to 21, omitting No 13.

Right: HIGH STREET, THE RUTLAND ARMS C1955 DETAIL FROM N23001

The inn covers a very large area. The gable facing the High Street has the arms of the Duke of Rutland displayed on it. The motto is 'Pour y Parvenir' - 'To attain'.

BURY ROAD

THE WAR MEMORIAL 1922 71928

As we can see from the cleanliness of this sculpture, it is new. Beyond the Clock Tower, at the beginning of the Bury Road on the left, is a small Memorial Garden. It is a tiny piece of the Severals fenced in by iron railings. It was constructed in memory of the men of Newmarket who fell in the Great War 1914-18. The actual memorial is a fine square column of grey granite surmounted by an urn. In June 2005 the names of those killed in the 1941 bombing of Newmarket were added to the memorial stone. The gardens were renovated.

THE JUBILEE CLOCK TOWER C1960 N23063

The War Memorial Gardens with its tall white column is to the left of the Clock Tower.

BURY ROAD

THE leafy avenue that is the Bury Road (see 71921 and 81962, page 58) is safe enough for the lady with the pram to walk down the side; perhaps the path was rather uneven. A handcart is directly in front of her, and a man is sweeping. The horses left manure on the roads, making them hazardous for pedestrians and cyclists alike, and there were several road sweepers employed in the 1920s. By 1929, a seat has been provided on the Severals (81962, left) and two men are taking advantage of it. A string of horses are walking slowly across the Severals. There are two cars just passing the Bury Heath, right, where most of the gallops are. Warren Hill can be seen in the distance.

Racehorses head up to the gallops (see 71918, page 59). One horse, on the right beyond the fence, is crossing the Bury Road to join the others on the heath. The large building behind the first horse in the string is the Drill Hall on the Snailwell Road. The men are all wearing caps and jackets, and have ties around their necks.

Newmarket is celebrated for its race meetings, studs, sales and racing establishments. These are frequented by visitors from all parts of the world.

BURY ROAD

Above: BURY ROAD 1922 71921

Right: RACEHORSES, MORNING EXERCISE 1922 71918

Below Left: BURY ROAD 1929 81962

Below Centre: THE GALLOPS, BURY-SIDE C1955 N23012
This view was taken looking toward Warren Hill.

Below Right: BURY ROAD C1965 N23070
No Parking signs and large lamp standards are now in place.

BURY ROAD

Right: HORSES AT EXERCISE 1922 71920

A string of horses are walking sedately near to the Bury Road.

Below: HORSES AT EXERCISE 1929 81964

Several strings of racehorses can be seen on the Bury Heath. The Jockey Club decides every morning which gallops can be used that day.

The Downs which enclose Newmarket are very suitable for horses; the underlying chalk ensures a good drainage. In the 17th and 18th centuries the races were matches between two horses, often ridden by the owner. Bets were placed and the races were much longer than at present, finishing almost where the Sir Daniel Cooper Memorial is today at the beginning of the High Street. Gradually the influence of the Jockey Club produced rules. Shorter distances with given weights for the horses to carry were introduced. By the 19th century horses were numbered, saddled in a specific place and paraded before the racegoers.

The Chapman Plan of the town in 1787 lists 19 stables, several still existing today. The owners included Their Royal Highnesses the Prince of Wales and the Duke of Cumberland, the Dukes of Queensberry, Chartres, Belton and Lord Clermont. Today some 50 plus training yards operate in Newmarket, from large modern ones to small but vibrant examples. Owners no longer ride their own horses; many are owned by wealthy arabs, who have brought prosperity to the area. There are in excess of 2,000 horses in training in the town. They have the use of 17 miles of artificial gallops, 40 miles of turf gallops as well as 30 miles of walking grounds and a considerable number of acres of woodland. The race meetings take place from Spring to Autumn. Two of the five Classic races take place on the Rowley Mile Racecourse, the 1,000 Guineas for 3 year old Fillies and the 2,000 Guineas for 3 year old Colts and Fillies but excluding Geldings.

The horses we see in N23055, pages 62-63, are just coming back from the top of Warren Hill, where they will have had a splendid panoramic view of Newmarket and its environs. Even this low down on the heath several places can be identified. The large three-storey house on the left is Osbourne House. It is often found in pictures painted by various artists in the 18th century. The first woman to train horses, Nellie Chaloner, trained at Osbourne House in the late 19th century. The elegant spire of St Mary's church can be seen above the roofs. On the right the leafy trees are lining the Bury Road, and at the extreme right is St Agnes's church.

BURY ROAD

Right: RACEHORSES CROSSING THE
MAIN ROAD C1955 N23036
*The triangle on the post is a warning
to beware.*

Below: RACEHORSES EXERCISING,
BURY-SIDE C1960 N23055
*Progress has been made; women
are riding out. From the edge of
the plantation on Warren Hill, the
Downs stretch into the distance.*

Below Right: RACEHORSES
EXERCISING, BURY-SIDE C1960 N23054

BURY ROAD

St Agnes' Church was built by the Duchess of Montrose as a memorial to her second husband, Stirling Crawfurd. He died in Cannes in 1883. When the mausoleum was finished in 1885, she had his body transported home. It arrived in Newmarket by train on a late November night. It was taken across the Heath and was interred at midnight; the Duchess, her close friend and the priest were the only people in attendance. The church is built in red brick with stone dressings in the Decorated style.

The Cottage Hospital (see 81959, pages 64-65) stands in Old Station Road, which branches left at the end of the Bury Road near to the Clock Tower. It was built in 1879 in memory of Admiral Rous, who had been a great patron of the turf. It was built in a Queen Anne style of architecture, entirely of red brick. The land was donated by Sir Richard Wallace, KCB (he died in 1890). The Jockey Club erected it at a cost of approximately £5,000, and they continued to maintain it. The complex consisted of almshouses for two married couples and six single persons, and also a hospital, built in a pavilion system and containing ten beds for men and boys. Principally it was for those employed in the racing industry. There were also four beds for women and two for private patients. The wards were named respectively after the Prince of Wales, Sir J D Astley, Sir James Lowther and Lord Hartingdon. It formed three sides of a quadrangle. The hospital continued in use until 1966; it was

BURY ROAD

then purchased by the local council and converted into homes for the elderly.

Returning to the High Street, we can take a look down Palace Street (88439, page 67), where we have the side of the Rutland Arms on the right. To the left we have a partial view of Nell Gwynne's House. It is 17th-century with two storeys, attics and five windows, but it was converted into three houses in the 19th century. It is timber-framed and rendered; there is a moulded wooden band at first floor level. The roof is pantiled, and the eaves soffit has a fretted pendant frieze. The windows we see here are mid 19th-century sash windows with architraves and wooden hoodmoulds; three have their original hinged louvered shutters. It is believed that the house was built for Nell Gwynne to use when she accompanied King Charles II to Newmarket. The car down on the right-hand side is parked outside Palace House. The gates opposite lead into Palace House stables. These are 17th-century and among the oldest stables in Newmarket; they were used by Charles II when he came here. At the bottom of the street rises the crenellated tower of All Saints' church (also see N23051).

THE ROUS MEMORIAL HOSPITAL 1929 81959

The clock on the cupola points to 10 to 12. The patients are outside in the fresh air - one appears to be still in bed, whilst three are in deck chairs nearby. Another person is in a wicker chair, with an empty wheelchair nearby; could this distinguish private patients from others?

BURY ROAD

Above: ALL SAINTS' CHURCH C1960 N23051

The tower of this church is orientated south-west, which is most unusual. The site was small, so the church had to be made to fit into it. The original medieval church, used by the court when they came to Newmarket in the 17th century, had become neglected by the mid 19th century. The old church was demolished, and a new one erected in 1876. It was decided to make it a memorial to the late Lord George Manners, the Lord of the Manor of Newmarket. It is a large, handsome Gothic structure, designed by W Oldham Chambers from Lowestoft. The three-tiered tower can be seen here, and one of the two aisles. The slated roof tops a structure of flint and limestone rubble, with Bath stone dressings. A small, neat wall surrounds the church.

Opposite: PALACE STREET 1938 88439

ORDNANCE SURVEY MAP

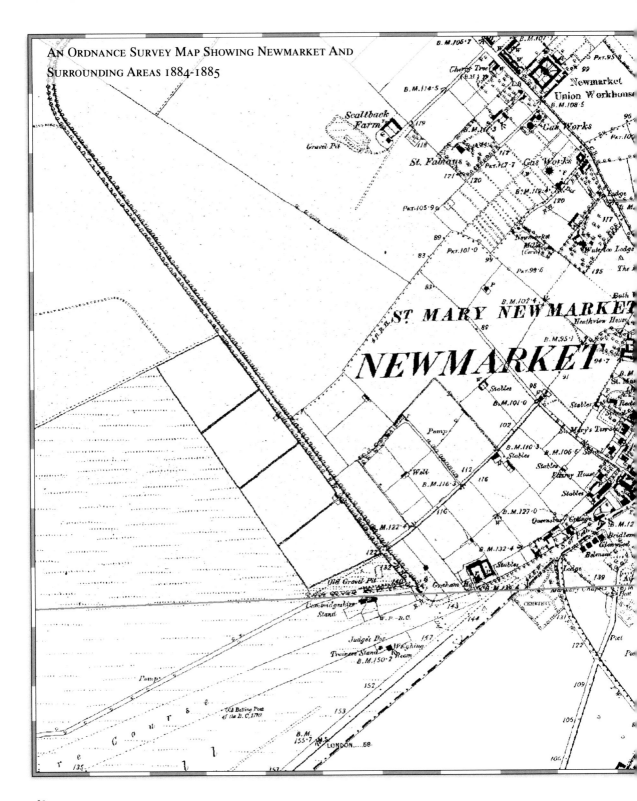

An Ordnance Survey Map Showing Newmarket And Surrounding Areas 1884-1885

BOTTOM OF THE HIGH STREET TO THE CAMBRIDGE ROAD

THE elevated part of the street on the immediate left of N23026 is known as The Terrace. It is lined with attractive late 18th- and early 19th-century houses. Originally built by patrons of the turf, they are now offices; they still carry the names of the previous owners, Clifton, Lonsdale, Richmond and Lushington - a reminder of a bygone age. The substantial iron railings ensure that no one plunges onto the High Street. The large tree at the top end of The Terrace is in the garden of Lord Wolverton. The house there was built as a family home for his father in 1898.

The wide street leads to the two race courses at Newmarket. The July Course, which is just beyond the Devil's Ditch, is the furthest away. The ditch is a seven-mile-long defensive earthwork of the 6th century, stretching from wooded Woodditton to Reach at the edge of the fens. The Rowley Mile is the nearer of the two courses. If we bear right at the monument just visible on the far side of the lorry travelling up the road, we come to the course. In the 1950s it was not unusual on race days to see racehorses being led up the High Street to go racing.

HIGH STREET C1955 N23026

Bottom of the High Street to the Cambridge Road

The right side of the street is a mixture of business and residential properties. Crisswell's garage is owned by a local family. It provides an AA service, and there are other signs showing what they are offering to the public (see N23026A).

This garage is also selling cars, the showroom being at the front. Playfords, the electricians are next door to the garage, another family business. The flats above both shops were rented out; the growth of Newmarket was just taking off at the time of N23026, and rented living premises were difficult to find. Playfords and the Black Bear stand at the junction of Black Bear Lane. The Black Bear is a hotel and public house, like most of the old inns in the town. On race days accommodation is at a premium, and many householders take in racegoers and sales people; this is just continuing in the same tradition established in Stuart times. The Black Bear is

selling and advertising Tolly Ales; today it is an Indian Restaurant. The houses beyond are residential, ending with the large bay-windowed Clarendon House. Just visible are some of the oldest stables in the town. The range comprises a mid 18th-century range of stables, now neglected and decaying, alas.

Clarendon House (see 71927, page 72, on the left) is an 18th-century two-storeyed house, with attics and a basement. It is built of red brick with a band of gauged brick at the first floor. It has a pantiled roof with flat-headed dormers. The windows have flat arches of gauged brick, flush frames and small-paned sashes, some having thick 18th-century glazing bars. The spearhead railings are early 19th-century, and there is a pedestrian gate leading to a set of stone steps. Residential houses continue down the High Street towards the Black Bear. Teas and luncheons are advertised on the other side of

Above Left and Above Centre: HIGH STREET, SIGNS ON CRISSWELL'S GARAGE
C1955 N23026A

Above Right and Left: THE TERRACE AND HIGH STREET 1922 71927B

Crisswell's Garage had a fine selection of signs on its frontage, including signs for the AA, Lucas Batteries and Vauxhall and Bedford cars, and in 1922 its own sign was splendidly ornate.

BOTTOM OF THE HIGH STREET TO THE CAMBRIDGE ROAD

Left: THE TERRACE AND HIGH STREET 1922
DETAIL FROM 71927

Below: THE TERRACE AND HIGH STREET 1922 71927

This is one of the most delightful views of Newmarket, and easily recognised today. The street here has withstood the changes of time. To take an almost identical picture today, you can stand on a nearby pedestrian island; it would protect you from the constant stream of traffic that flows through the town.

Right: HIGH STREET 1929 81958

The unsaddled horses being led down the High Street could be on their way to the sales ring at Tattersalls. The Avenue is just on the left; it leads directly to the sales paddocks.

Bottom of the High Street to the Cambridge Road

High Street 1938 88437

Across the road from the Masonic Club on the right is a little confectioner and tobacconists, E Fairweather. An advert for Players cigarettes is prominently displayed on a wall poster. The Doric Cinema, built in the 1930s, offers all modern facilities, including a car park, a lounge, and teas for those who prefer a comfortable modern setting in which to relax. Both the Doric and the Kingsway Cinemas are night clubs today.

Bottom of the High Street to the Cambridge Road

Black Bear Lane next to Crisswell's Garage. A postman's wheeled wicker basket is on the road by the post box, but there is no sign of the postman!

The landmark of the Carlton cupola can be seen against the skyline (see detail from 71927, page 72) - it is missing today. In the distance are the chalk downlands of the Bury Heath and Warren Hill - we can see perfectly the dry valley in which Newmarket nestles. Behind the red brick wall (71927, on the right) is the Wolverton family mansion house, Queensberry House, built in 1898 by Col R W Edis in the Queen Anne style. The architect was knighted in 1919. He designed most of the large houses in The Avenue, and The Coronation Hotel near the passenger station. He also did a great deal of architectural work in London. He used many 18th-century internal fittings that had been in a previous house on the site. An attractive lamp standard stands before the entrance to The Terrace. At this period, the fine houses are still residential. The war ended the viability of these large houses - their upkeep needed many servants. Today they are offices; Terrace House is the office of Tattersalls.

The building on the left of 81958, page 73, is the Masonic Club. It is a small extension of Godolphin House, which stands on the corner of The Avenue. It consists of one storey and is mid 18th-century with 20th-century alterations. The entrance is impressive. The door has six fielded panels, an architrave and an open Doric porch with entablature and a pediment on a pair of columns. There are some 18th-century spear-head railings along part of the street frontage. Like Clarendon House, it has mid 18th-century sash windows with flat arches of gauged brick and small-paned sashes with thick glazing bars. The Masonic Club is still thriving at this venue. The little boys in their short trousers and the window cleaner (right) are showing a great interest in the horses. The blind over the first shop on the right is printed with the information: 'Jessie Blyth, Milliner'. Hats in the 1920s were still part of a woman's every-day dress, with a special one for church or chapel on a Sunday. Those who belonged to the racing fraternity needed many more hats than most women, as race meetings tended to be fashion occasions as well as social events. A little lane comes next; it leads into Grosvenor Yard, which is full of small cottages, stables and the Grosvenor Arms - now called 'The Yard', this is an 18th-century building. On the other side of the lane is William Parker's jewellery and optician's shop. A small restaurant half-way up on the right provides teas and luncheons for those going to or from the races.

HIGH STREET C1955 N23027

The road sign stands before the Electricity Showrooms. The bypass has not yet been built, and all traffic comes through the town. Selright, a ladies' fashion store, is followed by Toppings shoe shop and then Anscome & Sons, photographers.

BEHIND THE NORTH SIDE OF THE HIGH STREET

MANY CHANGES to the Memorial Gardens, behind the Memorial Hall, have taken place over the years as fashions and needs have altered. The gardens were dug up during the war years, and several air-raid shelters were inserted. The 1950s and 60s saw more child-orientated facilities being introduced into public parks, and Newmarket Council responded with a paddling pool and a sand area (see N23057, pages 76-77). Many people of all ages are using the gardens; a sign shows that the lavatories are not far away. The lamp standard has the bars for a ladder in case the bulb needs changing or the light needs attention .The splendid steeple of St Mary's church, cedar shingled, with a leaded apex and a cockerel weather vane, dominates the skyline. The hedge in the background encloses a bowling green. Children are not permitted into this area (and nor are adults if they

HIGH STREET C1960 N23039

The entrances to the King Edward VII Memorial Gardens are on either side of the Hall.

are liable to walk on the grass!). Several swings are just out of sight on the right-hand side of the park.

The chapel of St Mary was built on this site some time between 1265 and 1283 by Sir Giles Argentein. He built it not only for piety but to serve the market-based community of the town - they were some way from their parish church at Exning. It did not become a parish church in its own right until the 16th century. The church we see today (N23058, page 80) had major structural changes made in the 15th and 19th centuries. The tower with its slim spire, and the beautiful tracery of the west window that we see here, are 15th-century. Most of the rest of the church dates from the 1850s restoration. The slated roof and the flint and rubble walls are very solid. During the restoration an exquisite 13th-century roofed and arched double piscina was uncovered; it is still used for the disposal of the water at the Eucharist.

The traffic has increased considerably by 1955 (see N23010, pages 78-79). On the right is the neat flint wall surrounding the cemetery. The original burial board was formed in 1859, and two mortuary chapels were built. The cemetery is cared for by the council today, and has recently been expanded. Many famous people are buried here, well-known names throughout the racing industry - for example, the jockey Fred Archer.

If we look at picture N23010, we will see Warren Hill in the background, where Warren Towers stands; this was the home of Sir Daniel Cooper and his wife Lady Harriet Cooper. Sir Daniel was a popular owner and a great benefactor to the town. He was an Australian by birth; his father was the first baronet, and

BEHIND THE NORTH SIDE OF THE HIGH STREET

Left: ST MARY'S CHURCH 1922 71931

It is thought that it is the old sanctus bell that hangs here; the small open wooden bell cot is probably of the 17th century.

Below Left: THE PADDLING POOL AND ST MARY'S CHURCH C1960 N23057

Below: THE COOPER MEMORIAL AND CAMBRIDGE ROAD 1929 81961

This memorial terminates the High Street at the Cambridge end. On the right-hand side of it is the road to the Rowley Mile Course; this area is known as Birdcage Walk. At one time the finishing post for the races stood here. In Stuart times a stand was erected on this spot, which brought the racing literally into the town. Behind the fence, large Victorian residential houses stand in gardens set well back from the road. Some also have stables attached, giving easy access to the heath.

he had been the Speaker of the New South Wales Legislative Assembly. Sir Daniel's brother William was a trainer in the town; Nat Flatman, a successful jockey, had been his apprentice. When Lady Harriet was deciding on a monument for her husband, she realised that she could see the beginning of the Cambridge Road from Warren Towers. She settled on this as the site for the Cooper Monument. Lady Cooper announced her plans and commissioned the architect E A Rickards to design a memorial. H Poole the sculptor was to fashion it, and White & Sons, a London firm of masons, were to construct it. It was finally in place by 1910, and all their names will be seen inscribed upon it. It has a fountain with an oval base, a curved, fluted and arched column on either side, and a canopy surmounted by a draped urn. The fountain head is in the shape of a sea shell. Travellers welcome the sight of it when returning to the town, just as they do the Clock Tower at the other end of the street.

Main Road c1955 N23010

St Mary's Church c1960 N23058

Below:

The Grandstand, Rowley Mile Racecourse 1922 71932

The stand is hardly big enough to hold the hundreds of people who arrive by train on race days, and they spread out onto the course between races. There are many complaints at the moment about the lack of facilities: the stand is single-storey, with limited covering for the racegoers. At the side is a hand-operated screen to give details of the horses, jockeys and positions. Today, however, a recent £16m refurbishment, opened by Her Majesty Queen Elizabeth II on 6 May 2000, has transformed it into a world-class facility.

The Rowley Mile Racecourse c1960 N23066

It is race day, and the stands are full of people. On the right is the Silver Ring, where the horses parade before going down to the start. This gives the public a chance to see what the horse behaves like with its jockey up. Betting only takes place on the stands side.

THE EXNING ROAD

FROM Wellington Street one ascends Mill Hill; Exning Road begins at the top of it. For hundreds of years, this road between Exning and Newmarket did not exist - the route went from the top of Mill Hill across the heath. Exning Road is a ribbon development which began with the Union Workhouse in 1837. It was situated about half-way between the two settlements.

The Exning Road Working Men's Club is on the immediate right of photograph N23018; a flag pole is in the grounds. The triangle on the post is warning people to be careful, as the entrance to the Hospital is only yards away. The gable of St Etheldreda's church can be seen in the trees. It was the church attached to the Poor Law Institution and is built of flint and stone. It was erected by voluntary contributions in 1895 at a cost of £600, and has seating for two hundred people. The Hospital entrance comes next. Originally the Union Workhouse, it was transformed into a hospital during the war and became part of the National Health Service on 5 July 1948. Known as White Lodge Hospital, it then became Newmarket General Hospital. Now it is an outpatients' hospital only. The fence on the left encloses the Gas Board's property.

The entrance to the Hospital (see N23013, pages 82-83) is near the chimney stack on the left without a chimney pot. On the opposite side of the road there is a bus shelter. The shop on the corner of the road junction is J Wheeler & Son, a grocer's, confectioner's and stationer's, and also the

EXNING ROAD AND THE HOSPITAL C1955 N23018

THE EXNING ROAD

Exning Road Post Office. There is a post box immediately outside the premises.

St Phillip's Road (see N23014, page 86), which leads off Exning Road by the Post Office, is a road of solid terraced houses. Built of brick with slate roofs, they have a feeling of substance about them. The tree on the right marks the position of St Phillip's church. It was an iron structure erected in 1893, with a nave and chancel, and seating for one hundred and fifty persons. It was demolished a few years ago, and houses have been built on the site.

New industries are entering the town. These factories (see N23019, page 87) are built on land that has been cleared beyond the council houses. Power Controls is an English company, and Magnetic Devices next to it is American. Amongst other things, they were producing solenoids for use in the popular new television sets.

The period from 1922 to 1960 has shown changes in some areas. There is a greater density of traffic in evidence than in the 1920s, and islands have been established to ensure the safety of pedestrians crossing the road. Horses no longer saunter on the High Street, which has white lines painted along it; with the increase of motor vehicles, bicycles have declined, and people are no longer wearing hats all the time. The street lighting has probably changed more times than anything else over the years. Many shops, though, are still family businesses, and the Market continues to be held on Tuesday and Saturday.

EXNING ROAD C1955 N23013

The Exning Road

EXNING ROAD AND POST OFFICE C1955 N23015

Beside Wheeler's Post Office on the opposite corner of St Phillip's Road is the Cherry Tree, selling Tolly Ale.

The Exning Road

Above: St Phillip's Road c1955 N23014

Below: King Edward VII Road c1955 N23017

The next road running parallel to St Phillip's is King Edward VII Road. The Gospel Hall is on the left, with a corner grocer's on the other side. A sign just inside says 'Join our Xmas Club'.

EXNING ROAD c1955 N23020

Most of these houses are early 20th century. Some of the very first council houses built in Newmarket stretch away into the distance.

POWER CONTROLS LTD FACTORY c1955 N23019

Names of Subscribers

The following people have kindly supported this book by purchasing limited edition copies prior to publication.

Dorothy Astill

For Bill Barton, in memory of the Barton and Grass families

Mrs B Bendall, in memory of The Bendalls

Derek Birch, Newmarket

Ray and Joyce Boreham, Exning

Mr & Mrs J D Braybrooke, Exning, Newmarket

In loving memory of Les Brooks, from all his family

The Buckell Family

Jim & Judy Bursford, Newmarket, from Cindy

The Chilcott Family, Newmarket

To David Courtman, my Dad, love you forever, Debs

Peter & Roslyn Cresswell, Peterhouse Drive

Arthur James Crickmere

John Dennis, Newmarket

Ms C F Eaton-Hall

Mr S Eley and Mrs I N Eley

Ray and Betty Elwood

John Edward Fenn

To my brother John Flood, in memory of our parents

Brenda Galer

In memory of my parents, Susan May Gardiner

For the Granger family of Newmarket

46 years in Newmarket, the Green family

Ruth Halsey

The Hansell Family

Margaret Joan Harrington

Brian G Heasman

Frank and Priscilla Hill, Newmarket 2006

FW Hobbs & Co Ltd, Ironmongers, Newmarket

Raymond Iles

Stewart & Mary Jacobs, our beginning 1969

In memory of June Jaggard, Newmarket

Roy Jamieson, in memory of my parents

For Mum and Dad, love Jane

To Anne, in memory of my friendship with Joan

To Katarzyna, love Wendy, Lara and Eve x

Edward Last

Mrs J Litten

To Kathleen Miller from the Rolfe Family

Mrs Christine (Tonge) Muller of Newmarket

Newmarket Journal

To Olivia & Grace, love Nana & Opa

The Peck Family, Nat Flatman St, Newmarket

Douglas Owen Pitches

Iain Pountain, resident since 1948

Alasdair Pountain, 60 years old 9/10/06

Edward Price

Anthony H Pringle, Newmarket, 13/4/1938

Eileen Protheroe (Crozier family)

To my children Shane, Ryan and Jasmine, Newmarket

John Sharp, memories of the Sharp Family

Simon Spence

Robert Spence

Geoff Timmins

To Marjory Walker, love Lynn and Ernie

George Walsh

Mollie Anne Watson, Newmarket, 17/12/1939

Ann Williamson, Nat Flatman Street

Index

FRITH PRODUCTS & SERVICES

Francis Frith would doubtless be pleased to know that the pioneering publishing venture he started in 1860 still continues today. Over a hundred and forty years later, The Francis Frith Collection continues in the same innovative tradition and is now one of the foremost publishers of vintage photographs in the world. Some of the current activities include:

INTERIOR DECORATION

Today Frith's photographs can be seen framed and as giant wall murals in thousands of pubs, restaurants, hotels, banks, retail stores and other public buildings throughout the country. In every case they enhance the unique local atmosphere of the places they depict and provide reminders of gentler days in an increasingly busy and frenetic world.

PRODUCT PROMOTIONS

Frith products are used by many major companies to promote the sales of their own products or to reinforce their own history and heritage. Frith promotions have been used by Hovis bread, Courage beers, Scots Porage Oats, Colman's mustard, Cadbury's foods, Mellow Birds coffee, Dunhill pipe tobacco, Guinness, and Bulmer's Cider.

GENEALOGY AND FAMILY HISTORY

As the interest in family history and roots grows world-wide, more and more people are turning to Frith's photographs of Great Britain for images of the towns, villages and streets where their ancestors lived; and, of course, photographs of the churches and chapels where their ancestors were christened, married and buried are an essential part of every genealogy tree and family album.

FRITH PRODUCTS

All Frith photographs are available Framed or just as Mounted Prints and Posters (size 23 x 16 inches). These may be ordered from the address below. Other products available are - Address Books, Calendars, Jigsaws, Canvas Prints, Postcards and local and prestige books.

THE INTERNET

Already ninety thousand Frith photographs can be viewed and purchased on the internet through the Frith websites and a myriad of partner sites.

For more detailed information on Frith products, look at this site:
www.francisfrith.com

See the complete list of Frith Books at: www.francisfrith.com
This web site is regularly updated with the latest list of publications from The Francis Frith Collection. If you wish to buy books relating to another part of the country that your local bookshop does not stock, you may purchase on-line.

For further information, trade, or author enquiries please contact us at the address below:
The Francis Frith Collection, Unit 6, Oakley Business Park, Wylye Road, Dinton, Wiltshire SP3 5EU.
Tel: +44 (0)1722 716 376 Fax: +44 (0)1722 716 881 Email: sales@francisfrith.co.uk

---

See Frith products on the internet at www.francisfrith.com

FREE PRINT OF YOUR CHOICE
CHOOSE A PHOTOGRAPH FROM THIS BOOK
+ £3.80 POSTAGE

Mounted Print
Overall size 14 x 11 inches (355 x 280mm)

TO RECEIVE YOUR FREE PRINT

Choose any Frith photograph in this book

Simply complete the Voucher opposite and return it with your remittance for £3.50 (to cover postage and handling) and we will print the photograph of your choice in SEPIA (size 11 x 8 inches) and supply it in a cream mount ready to frame (overall size 14 x 11 inches).

Order additional Mounted Prints at HALF PRICE - £12.00 each (normally £24.00)

If you would like to order more Frith prints from this book, possibly as gifts for friends and family, you can buy them at half price (with no additional postage costs).

Have your Mounted Prints framed

For an extra £20.00 per print you can have your mounted print(s) framed in an elegant polished wood and gilt moulding, overall size 16 x 13 inches (no additional postage required).

IMPORTANT!

❶ Please note: aerial photographs and photographs with a reference number starting with a "Z" are not Frith photographs and cannot be supplied under this offer.

❷ Offer valid for delivery to one UK address only.

❸ These special prices are only available if you use this form to order. You must use the ORIGINAL VOUCHER on this page (no copies permitted). We can only despatch to one UK address.

❹ This offer cannot be combined with any other offer.

As a customer your name & address will be stored by Frith but not sold or rented to third parties. Your data will be used for the purpose of this promotion only.

Send completed Voucher form to:

**The Francis Frith Collection,
19 Kingsmead Business Park, Gillingham,
Dorset SP8 5FB**

Voucher for FREE and Reduced Price Frith Prints

Please do not photocopy this voucher. Only the original is valid, so please fill it in, cut it out and return it to us with your order.

Picture ref no	Page no	Qty	Mounted @ £12.00	Framed + £20.00	Total Cost £
		1	Free of charge*	£	£
			£12.00	£	£
			£12.00	£	£
			£12.00	£	£
			£12.00	£	£
			£12.00	£	£

*Please allow 28 days for delivery.
Offer available to one UK address only*

* Post & handling		£3.80
Total Order Cost		£

Title of this book . . . .

I enclose a cheque/postal order for £ . . . . made payable to 'The Francis Frith Collection'

OR please debit my Mastercard / Visa / Maestro card, details below

Card Number:

Issue No (Maestro only):   Valid from (Maestro):

Card Security Number: Expires:

Signature:

Name Mr/Mrs/Ms . . . .

Address . . . .

. . . .

. . . .

. . . . Postcode . . . .

Daytime Tel No . . . .

Email . . . .

Valid to 31/12/18

Free Print – see overleaf

Can you help us with information about any of the Frith photographs in this book?

We are gradually compiling an historical record for each of the photographs in the Frith archive. It is always fascinating to find out the names of the people shown in the pictures, as well as insights into the shops, buildings and other features depicted.

If you recognize anyone in the photographs in this book, or if you have information not already included in the author's caption, do let us know. We would love to hear from you, and will try to publish it in future books or articles.

An Invitation from The Francis Frith Collection to Share Your Memories

The 'Share Your Memories' feature of our website allows members of the public to add personal memories relating to the places featured in our photographs, or comment on others already added. Seeing a place from your past can rekindle forgotten or long held memories. Why not visit the website, find photographs of places you know well and add YOUR story for others to read and enjoy? We would love to hear from you!

www.francisfrith.com/memories

Our production team

Frith books are produced by a small dedicated team at offices near Salisbury. Most have worked with the Frith Collection for many years. All have in common one quality: they have a passion for the Frith Collection.

Frith Books and Gifts

We have a wide range of books and gifts available on our website utilising our photographic archive, many of which can be individually personalised.

www.francisfrith.com